THE ART OF SELF-RELIANCE

A TIMELESS SECRET TO SUCCESS

SUKHPREET SINGH

Editing
Lloyd Thompson-Taylor, USA
www.dragonrealmpress.com

Formatting
Jamie Culican, USA
www.dragonrealmpress.com

Cover Design
Jeya Ananth Velusamy, India
www.behance.net/jeyananth

Author Photograph
Geln Morrison, Dubai

CONTENTS

To my adorable wife and lovely daughters.

EPIGRAPH

*"The world turns aside to let any man pass,
who knows where he is going."*
-Epictetus-

PREFACE

"It's been a year and still I don't forget the sound of those three words. The words which became the source of constant agony in my heart and mind. Three words which didn't let me sleep peacefully. It doesn't matter how deep I dive into my work, how much I try to run away, but the pain of those three words doesn't go away. Maybe because those have been said by someone very close to me. Someone who can simply walk through the emotional walls I have built around myself. Someone who has spent so much time with me, that understands me more than myself. Those three words, which I can't erase from my memory.

I still vaguely remember the ambience, the time, the venue, and the simplicity with which he said, "You have changed."

I laughed when I heard them. Said a cliché, change is the law of nature. But he insisted. But you were not like all of us, he said. You were special. You were brave. You were a free bird. You were the chosen one. But now, you are just like us. A face in the crowd. Even your presence or absence is meaningless. What a shame. Even you have changed.

Perhaps, it's not the pain of the words that torment my soul. Rather, it's the pain of my friend's shattered expectations that bother me the most. I guess the only way to placate the pain, is to become the person I was supposed to be. I think, at last, it's time to become the real me."

In my 15 years of journey in the corporate world, I have seen many intelligent and promising people just fade away into the oblivion. People who started their career with a dream, with a fire in their belly, with a desire to make an impact, simply turned into empty suits, melancholically participating in the race towards the horizon.

All their personal dreams and naive ambitions turned into dust over time. I always used to wonder, what happened? Why, though successful as per the world's "living standards," did they still fail to achieve their full potential? They could have been much more, but they settled for much less. Though they were achievers, they were still running away from the hollowness of their lives. The flame within, which was supposed to burn brighter than the Sun, ended up being a candle, melting away into the river of time.

The *eureka* moment came to me when I also fell into same league. Personal dreams were traded for the high-flying life of the corporate world. The fire to make an impact was outshined by the glitter of materialistic things. Hiding behind the curtains of worldly roles and responsibilities and shying away from the challenge of pursuing my true self. Standing there alone, pondering the difference between where I wanted to be and where I have reached. Reflecting on the journey I have taken and the paths I have abandoned. Why did it happen? How can I turn the tide? How can I be what I was supposed to be? I found the answer. The solution. I found the key.

The key to unlocking a world of opportunities. The key to unlocking a treasure trove of happiness. The key to unlocking the future.

This book carries the details of the key. It also shows how anyone can get the key. Before you proceed further, I must advise you that this is not a story book. There is no rag to riches story. This is not a compilation of interviews or an encyclopedia of famous quotes. This book is not for the people reading one book after another to find solace in dreaming about their future but refrain from taking any action. This is not for the whiners, for the quitters, or for the knowledge collectors.

This book is for the people standing on the verge of creating their dream lives and wondering how to start. It's for the innocent mind who has not yet sold his soul to the materialistic pursuits. It's for the one who has still not given up on his dreams for short-term success. It's for the one who still tries to listen to his internal voice, despite his mind being covered with clouds of fear and doubt.

This book is about the most fulfilling journey of one's life. It's about creating the future. It's about being the very best. It's about building a legacy for generations to come. This book is the key to unlock your true future. Nothing more, nothing less.

———

INTRODUCTION

ON A BRIGHT sunny day, it stood still. It was definitely an anomaly to the surroundings. Its presence was being noticed by everyone with a surprise. Everyone wondered at its presence, discussing the irregularities among themselves. Some were amazed by its presence and some were concerned. But there it was. Standing tall and casting its shadow beyond its reach.

It was an old Sidr tree. In middle of the desert, it stood several meters high, deeply rooted to weather droughts and floods, its beautiful yellow fruits turning red, representing maturity. Its presence in this environment was an act of defiance. It did not pay heed to the lack of water, harsh sun, gusty winds, nor shifting sands. Ages ago, the tree decided to be there, despite everything; none of the challenges mattered. Now, it provides shade to many living beings in the surroundings and an occasional respite to the travelers. Its absence wouldn't have meant anything to anyone, but its presence added a new dimension. As a living symbol of self-reliance.

———

DEFINING SELF-RELIANCE

SELF-RELIANCE IS FREEDOM. It's the freedom from the burden of becoming a replica of someone else. It's the freedom to become anything you desire or choose to be. It's the freedom to pursue any talent. It's the freedom to develop any skill. It's the freedom to choose your own battles. It's the freedom to make your own choices. It's the freedom to form your own opinions. It's the freedom to do things that matter. It's the freedom to be alive.

Self-reliance is hope. It's the sunshine that thaws a frozen heart. It's the spring to the withered mind. It's the star that gives directions to the lost dreams. It's the wind in the sails of the ship of our lives. It's the fuel that keeps us warm during the coldest night. It's the light that leads our way beyond our sight.

Self-reliance is belief. Belief in your capabilities and in your determination. Belief that you can create the world you have dreamed of. Belief that you can become the one you want to be. Belief that nothing is beyond your grasp. No obstacle is too big to overcome, no dream is too big to realise. Belief that you have a purpose and you have everything you need to materialise it.

Self-reliance is an expression. It's about expressing how you truly feel about things and about how you truly want to be. It's like walking tall without masks, without fear of other people's judgements. Not only is it about showing your strengths, it's also about not shying away from your weaknesses. It's about living truly. It's being your own avatar. Your own guiding star.

Self-reliance is power derived from within. Neither acquired nor inherited, the power of self-reliance stays with your regardless of circumstance. It makes you the master of your own destiny. It gives you control. It lets you to shape your own future. It's the power to face your demons, overcome your biggest fears, and build your own legacy.

Self-reliance is your shield against the naysayers, procrastinators, against the unambitious, against the misleaders and everyone else who takes pleasure in tearing you down. It will protect you and guide you as you become the man you were born to be. It will act as the steady rhythm, sounding strong through the cacophony of this world's cries. You will be a stallion amongst the herd.

Self-reliance should not be confused with individualism. Self-reliance is taking responsibility for one's life and making focused efforts to realize one's dreams. Self-reliance is acknowledging how things are and believing you have the capability to change them. Self-reliant people are the vanguards of hope, innovators, explorers, and creators of the world. They show the world a new way, a new direction. They believe in the collective good.

When you choose to embrace self-reliance, it becomes the fuel for the fire that burns within you. It carries you through the toughest times and the darkest nights. Nothing seems to stand in your way. The coldest night is not cold enough to freeze your way; the darkest hour is not dark enough to hide your view. The largest problems become just pebbles in your way. The oceans of doubts will be just droplets on your face. You will move forward, and the world will stand and watch you with awe.

———

THE POWER OF SELF-RELIANCE

IN LIFE, you have two simple choices. Sit and cry for not having things you desire or get out and work hard to get them. If you are part of the majority, who would rather sit and cry and complain about how hard it is to succeed, you can quit reading this book. This is not for people like you. If you are someone who wants to change his circumstances, who is determined to get the life he dream of and who wants to takes full responsibility of his life, this is the book for you.

How will you move forward when the situation is really tough and despite your best efforts, you are not able to find a break through? How will you make progress when the closest people don't show up to help you? How will you succeed when you don't see the light at the end of the tunnel, when you don't see an end to the darkness? How can you survive when your whole life is falling apart, when you are stuck in despair and have lost all hope?

There is only one thing that will get you through the toughest hour. One thing that, will not only put breeze under your wings of dreams, but also take you towards the end of your journey. One thing that will hold your hand in wilderness of fears. One thing that will take you towards light. One thing that will bring out the best in you.

It's your Self-reliance. The moment you embrace it, the struggles and hardships and roadblocks that surround you will look like solutions. You will find that needle in a haystack. You will walk on fire and float on water. But this enlightenment can only begin once you realize you have to rely on yourself. You have to take charge. You have to take control. You have to make a choice. You have to take action.

Life is too short. No one will simply hand you a million dollars and tell you to go live your dream. You must work hard. You must slough through the muck day and night. You must make your blood and sweat as one.

People will tell you, why something cannot be done. They will resent you when you insist otherwise. They will highlight all the challenges you will face. They will dump their own excuses on you and try their best to keep you down. If you want to break free from the chains of their circumstances and misconceptions, you must rely on yourself. The moment you depend on others for your dreams and goals, they will drag you down and keep you there until you forget yourself and become part of the crowd.

There is no saviour coming out of the stone; there is no philanthropist loaded with cash coming down your way; there is no miracle waiting to happen. It's only you and your efforts that will move the mountains your troubles have become. So, stop wishing and hoping against hope, that things will change on their own. They won't. Your self-reliance is the key.

If you want to make your mark, if you want to make your life worth it, if you seek freedom, follow your instincts. Do what you've always desired to. Break free from the current structure of society, rules, and mundane living. Step outside of the crowd and start your own journey. Reach towards the unknown, trusting only your instincts and your capabilities. Remove even the smallest grain of thought that you can piggyback on someone else's success. Rely on yourself.

There is a misconception, popularised by the followers, who had long given up on their dreams and silenced their inner voice, that you should monitor the success of others and try to replicate their journey. Do what others have done. They will preach you rag to riches stories; they will show you people who have gone through severe physical and mental challenges. They will blindfold you with the success of other people. They will sell you lies, wrapped around the truth, just to make you believe and follow them.

The truth is, you have a mind which has evolved over centuries. Your instincts are sharper than others. Your circumstances are different from anyone else's. It's only you, and your reliance on yourself, that will take you through. You were born to write your own story, create your own path. Don't fall into the trap of trying to rewrite others' stories and failing to be anything but yourself.

Never look up at the rich and successful in expectation of receiving their generosity. Don't rely on luck or miracles. Have faith in yourself and work hard to achieve what you want to achieve. You were born a winner so, don't be fooled into becoming a loser. Your circumstances will change. You will achieve things you aspire for. You will leave a legacy. All you have to do is believe in yourself and rely on yourself.

People who build their careers and characters with self-reliance will always be humble. They know the value of effort; they respect hard work. They know how difficult it is to be your own man. And these are the people who set an example. These are the people who leave an indelible mark on everyone they meet. These are the ones, who made their live worth living.

So, stop wasting your time, aspiring to be like someone

else and hoping to receive someone's help. Get up and start moving. Your family and friends are there to support you. But they cannot walk the path for you. You must seek out your goals, wherever that journey leads you. It's your responsibility. Only you can shoulder it.

Life is too short if you enjoy it and is too long if you drag through it. Things won't change by dreaming and hoping. They will only change through decisive action and persistent output of effort. You don't have to rely on others. Your instincts are enough to guide you.

Collect as much knowledge as possible, learn as many new skills as needed, and, in the end, use your own instinct and pursue your own dreams. Don't waste time replicating the actions of others. Be your own light and write your own story. There is no one else like you and there will never be. You are the only you, so make it count.

THE EFFECTS OF SELF-RELIANCE

ONCE YOU START practicing self-reliance you not only transform yourself but everything around you. It has a domino effect on your life and circumstances. Everything starts following your lead. Luck, fate, circumstance, everything waits for your direction. You become the guiding light.

It all starts with the simple act of accepting yourself and deciding to follow your dreams, despite every possible challenge. Afterwards, the struggle becomes the journey, the pain becomes the reward, the dream becomes the destination, and happiness becomes life. No obstacles or challenges matter during your pursuit to become your true self.

You are freed from the thoughts, expectations, preachings, and perceptions of those around you. It's the act of freeing your soul from the burden of unwanted things that propels you forward. Things that don't add value to your happiness but are checklist items for others. Your spirits are lifted.

The moment you accept responsibility, of your past, your present, and your future, you stand out from the crowd. You will start thinking freely and start questioning the boundaries imposed on yourself. For the first time, you will start thinking for yourself. You will start putting in real effort to realise your own dreams. You will stop being part of the rat race, an open case of the endless chase.

You will stop believing in excuses or rational thoughts as the reason for your current state. You will accept them. You will respect them. And then you will face them head on. You will move forward, not because of their absence but, despite their presence. it's your effort alone that will take you through this journey. The rough seas or the deserted lands, are just the temporary phases, they will pass by.

People will look at you in an awe, initially shocked, and then surprised by your flight. When you start to be yourself and break the mould, people will despise you, criticize you, and dislike you. They won't believe you. They will see you as an outsider in their guarded garden. A weed that will destroy the balance of the ecosystem. But once you persist, then they will follow you; they will copy you and they will dream to be you.

———

WHO SHALL PRACTICE SELF-RELIANCE?

AS AN INDIVIDUAL, who chose not to have a vegetative life, who chose not to live and die as a plant, who don't want to be a small grain of sand in the desert, Self-reliance is the panacea. The difference between the follower and the creator is the difference between living under one's existing conditions and finding the solutions to uplift themselves and those around them.

Self-reliance is the most important tool that leaders use to break away from the shackles of the past. It's at the core of the winner's mindset. The explorers who search for a different world, the builders who create the largest monuments, the travelers who trek beyond the stars, all live lives of self-reliance. It's the philosophy of an alchemist. Every problem the believers of this philosophy touch turns into a solution. It becomes a step on a staircase to success. It becomes a milestone.

Self-reliance is crucial not only for an individual's growth but also for businesses. Businesses that seek solutions to unattended problems, businesses that want to change their approach to current issues, businesses that want to innovate in order to remain relevant, all rely on self-reliance.

As a company, you can't afford to wait for others to develop a technology that will make your product better; you must do it own your own. You can't afford to risk being held at ransom for the critical component for your products and solutions. Develop your own supply chain and invest in research and development. Develop alternative sources of revenue. Invest in yourself to stay ahead of the competition.

Many companies go into vertical integration due to supply chain challenges. They don't wait for the market to play out and settle everything for them. They take initiative and become self-reliant. The companies who aim for long-term survival and success never endanger their existence by placing it in the hands of the others.

The companies who don't want to live under the shadow of the gigantic corporations, the companies who don't want to be followers of the market trends, the companies who don't want to be miniscule players in their area of impact, understand that self-reliance is the key. It's just like individuals. You can't be dependent on others. You must get up and fix things yourself. The companies built on this mindset are strongly positioned to weather the storms of a changing market. They will adapt fast and rebound faster. They will not only attune to market dynamics, they will also transform them. They will be the ones who become legendary.

Countries fed up with the imposed title of third world or the underdeveloped countries, need to take the development initiatives own their own. They can't keep relying on the charity of world aid organizations controlled by a few nations. These countries need to become self-reliant in developing and building their own resources.

These countries need to find their own ways to explore and use the available natural resources. They need to find ways to educate the population. They need to find ways to build infrastructure. They need to find ways to build an organised economy. If they keep on relying on other nations to help them, these countries will stay where they were or perhaps become event worst. One day, the helping nations will get tired of assisting and call it a day. Avoiding that future is absolutely in the hands of these countries. Once they build their economy, they can be free from the burden of other nation's pity.

The things that you build on your own, the foundation that you lay own your own, will be stronger and last longer. Building self-reliance among its citizens, among its development plans is critical for the growth. You must be your own master.

For thousands of years, our ancestors have relied on their instincts, knowledge, and skill to lay the foundation of the world we live in today. They discovered the art of lighting and controlling fire. They discovered the art of producing the food in a central location. They found ways to communicate with each other. They developed ways to track the time and they found ways of utilizing their natural resources.

Imagine if they have just hoped and relied on outside forces for their survival and growth; where we would have been. It's in our DNA to become better than we were born. To take our generation a step forward. To be self-reliant and create solutions. It's all within us.

Civilizations, countries, companies, and individuals share many traits. They are not built on false hope. They are not built on fantasies and fairy tales. They are built on actions and initiatives. They are built on tackling challenges head on. They are built on the refusal to accept the current state of things as final. They are built on visions of a better future. They are built on determination. They are built on corporation. Cooperation between two strong parties bringing their strengths on the board to build a better future.

Life doesn't provide us all of the tools when we start, but it does give us the ability to find solutions. It's our job to take what we're given and combine it. We must take one plus one and make two We have to find the solutions to seemingly unsolvable problems. We must become resourceful. We must rely on ourselves to create our future.

Always remember, the vanguards of hope are not the followers, they can't live with the world that others have created. They can't simply sit and complain how bad things are. They refuse to accept excuses for the current state of things. They rely on themselves to find the necessary solutions. They don't take no for an answer. They know that setbacks are only temporary. They know failing once doesn't means the end of the world. They know and believe, if anyone could do it, they could.

———

HOW TO BECOME SELF-RELIANT

MANY PEOPLE DREAM of reaching the stars, more dream of leaving a lasting impact, even more dream about living a fulfilling life. Among those brave hearts, the vanguards of hope, the chosen ones, the only common factor found in those who reach their dreams is the realization that nothing will happen on its own. The solutions will not fall from the sky, the mountains will not move own their own, the oceans will not divide. You must take an action and you have to find a solution. You must be self-reliant.

This brings us to the biggest question, how to become self-reliant?

Self-reliance can be achieved by following A.C.E. methodology. It's a three-step approach towards realizing your full potential and creating the life you deserve. It starts with:

1. **Acceptance** - This is the foundation. It explains why and how we must accept ourselves as we truly are and take responsibility for our life's journey. It's

about putting down the masks and setting aside ego. It's about discovering ourselves, coming to terms with reality, and finding peace at heart.

2. **Creation** - As the name states, it's the creator's stage. It guides us, shows us how we can shape our lives, based on our dreams and unique strengths. It teaches us how to overcome our inhibitions and take action, so we can create the future we aspire to and deserve.

3. **Embrace** - This is the sustenance stage. It shares the importance of being original and how hard work complemented with intelligence can sustain us on our journey to pursue our dreams. It teaches us how we can keep moving forward, despite all the challenges.

These stages need to be completed in sequential order, as each lays the foundation for the next stage. In the upcoming chapters, we discuss these stages in detail. These three stages will guide you as you become self-reliant and achieve your dreams.

———

STAGE ONE - ACCEPTANCE

NO TWO THUMBPRINTS are the same. No two hearts beat the same. You are unique. Your problems, your challenges, your demons, and your struggles are your own. Just like your dreams, your hopes, and your pursuits are your own. You may share certain similarities with those around you, but at your core, you are inherently different. Your journey is unique to you.

You cannot copy other people's steps; you cannot fill another person's shoes. Even attempting to think the same thoughts as another person is a recipe for failure. Learn from others, but don't replicate them. They are living their own journey. You have yours to complete. It's your path, and only you can walk it. Don't rely on the support of others. Rely on yourself. You are born with the knowledge and guided by the inner star; you will reach your destination.

PART A: DISCOVERING AND ACCEPTING YOURSELF

Acceptance is a purification process. It's the ultimate form of self-awareness. It's understanding what you can do and what you cannot. What you are good at and what you struggle with. What you enjoy and what you despise. Acceptance is a discovery and acknowledgment of yourself. The path to finding your true self and making peace with your past begins there.

Acceptance of oneself is a first step towards becoming self-reliant. It seems simple, but it requires deep self-exploration. It needs you to surrender your ego. It needs you to put down the mask. It needs you to acknowledge your limitations. It needs you to understand yourself. It needs you to listen to your inner voice.

Acceptance frees our souls from the burden of worldly expectations; it sets us aside from the mad race to be better than others, the rush to acquire more materialistic things than we need. It makes us light and enable us to focus on the things that truly matters. It helps us to see things in a different perspective. It helps us understand the life cycles of our past, make sense of our present, and grants us the freedom to shape our futures.

Now, it's time to discover yourself. Get a pen and a couple of blank sheets of paper. Move to a quiet place. We will go through the 4 steps of learning about ourselves. Towards the end of each step, there is a small exercise. Complete the task alone, without any inputs from others.

STEP 1 - FACE YOUR FEARS

To accept yourself, you must first lay out your fears. You need to identify and acknowledge the demons in your thoughts. Fear is a very strong force. It makes people do things they otherwise wouldn't dare do. At the same time, fear will hold you back when you must take a leap forward. Once you know your fears and understand how influential they are, only then you will know how to handle them.

Now, use the pen and paper to list all your fears. Title your sheet of paper, "The Fears" Then write down all the fears that come to your mind. There is no time limit, word limit, or word count. Don't overthink. Don't judge yourself. Let the thoughts flow. Just write down all fears that come to your mind. Be it about yourself, your family, friends, work, finances, health, etc. Anything that comes to your mind when you think about fear.

Keep writing until you've listed all the fears that come to mind. Once you're done, move the list to the side. Don't read it.

STEP 2 - ACKNOWLEDGE YOUR LIMITATIONS

After meeting your fears, you need to know your limitations. No two superheroes are the same. Every one of us is different. Acknowledging your limitations will help you identify your strengths. It's critical that you understand what you can and cannot do. You can't keep on blaming yourself for things beyond your control. You need to put down your mask and truly understand yourself.

Now, return to your pen and paper. Title it, "The Limitations." Take time to think about your limitations. Focus on the things you can't do well. For example, you might be a great public speaker when it comes to friends and family, but you struggle to find words in front of strangers or large groups. This part might take some time, so relax and keep writing down your limitations. One more example, you could be very keen about health and fitness, but you can't get out of bed early in the morning. Try to go through different facets of your life and think about things you really can't do.

Once again, do not read the list after finishing it. Keep it along with the previous list and move on to the third step.

STEP 3 - HIGHLIGHT YOUR STRENGTHS

When you know your fears and your limitations, you will understand what is holding you back. Now, it's time to identify your strengths. Irrespective of what you might think, all of us have unique strengths. Knowing your limitations is important, but it's more critical to know your strengths. Your strengths will differentiate you from others. Your strengths will define you, shape you, and lay the foundation of your future. Your strengths are the reservoir that you can always dip into and rely on.

It's time again to get back to the pen and paper. Write down "My Strengths" on top of the newest piece of paper. Before you start writing your strengths, keep in mind that you must only write down the strength you actually have; do not include those you wish you had. For example, you may be a slow decision maker, but you are persistent when following up once a decision has been made. In this case, you would write down persistence as your strength.

After writing down all your strengths, keep the list along with other sheets. Now it's time to move to the fourth step.

STEP 4 - EXPRESS YOUR DREAMS

Once you are done with knowing your fears, your limitations, and strengths, it's time to think about your real dreams, those thoughts that bring a sparkle to your eye. The dreams you let the voices of your naysayers drown. Dreams, which you have silently given up. We all had dreams when we were children. By the time we grow up, only a chosen few have lived out their dreams. The rest of us bury them by pursuing practical careers and stable lives. It's vital that you rediscover your dreams, all the dreams that you abandoned or tucked away. If you continue to ignore them, they will haunt you until your deathbed. Don't run from your dreams. Acknowledge them and work to fulfill them.

It's time again to return to pen and paper. Title this sheet "My Dreams." Take a break and let your mind wander back to your childhood. What you wanted to become. What you wanted to have. How you wanted your life to look. The kind of legacy you would like to leave. Think freely and write down everything that comes to your mind. Use short sentences. No details or action plans required. Write down your dreams until you've gotten everything out.

Once you are done writing down your dreams, bring all the papers together. It's time to get a glimpse of yourself. Start with your dreams. Go through the list and relate which of your strengths can help you fulfill your dreams. Then compare your dreams to your limitations to identify which limitations you must overcome to achieve your dreams. At this point, try to relate your limitations to your fears, so you can understand which fear is responsible for which limitation. Sometimes, you must address the fear to overcome the limitation.

These four steps will give you a holistic picture of yourself. In these words, the real you will be reflected. Knowing yourself is a very personal journey. Acknowledging your fears and your limitations breaks your ego and your pretentiousness. It makes you modest. Makes you humble. Makes you human. Knowing your strengths, and recognizing your dreams, give you motivation, hope, and direction for your future journey. You know what challenges need to be faced and what resources you must rely on. It's like looking at a clear sky after the clouds disperse, the first ray of sun touching your skin after the thunderstorm. Feeling the first fresh breeze of spring after a cold winter. You will meet your new self, the self you have buried for so long.

Once you have discovered yourself and accepted your

strengths, you will see yourself differently. You will stop criticizing yourself. You will stop relying on the opinions of others. Once you accepted the way you are, you will stop getting misled by the world. You will no longer pay any heed to the thoughts and impressions of others. You will know yourself and stand your ground. You will no longer be a stranger to yourself.

It's the knowledge of yourself that relaxes your heart and mind, that provides a pivot point to your wandering soul. Once you know yourself, determining which areas of your life to focus on to attain your goals is simple.

———

PART B: ACCEPTING THE THREE PHASES OF YOUR LIFE

The fact that we humans split our life's journey into past, present, and future is just for our brain's convenience. At the end of the day, the further our journey takes us, the greater our responsibility is to shape it. Self-reliance requires us to make choices. The lack of decision-making is more dangerous to our goals than making the wrong choice. So, you must decide where to head to next and begin taking steps in that direction.

All your dreams and your desires are within your reach. All you must do is take a step forward. Irrespective of your actions, the days will pass, the seasons will change, and the future will become the past. What happens, how it will happen, all depends upon you. This is such a powerful concept, that once you grasp the importance of this, you will always be where you want to be.

STEP 1 - THE PAST IS IN THE PAST

Once you understand yourself it's time to acknowledge and respect your past. Today, whatever you are, your past has played an important role in your development. Your thoughts, your actions, and your hesitations reflect your past. Your soul carries the shadows of your past. Never despise your past. It's the foundation of your today. It's the cornerstone of your building, the key to its stability. It's a seed which has burst and blossomed into today.

Your past could be very challenging or could be very fun. Either way, we need to respect it. Everything that happened in the past had an impact on your present. That game you lost, the promotion you couldn't get, the college you didn't get into, the scholarship you missed, the loved one you lost, the wrong decisions you made, they have all played a critical role on your present. You wouldn't be here without those events. They have carved their impression on your mind. They have cast their shadow on your thoughts. They have moulded you into what you are today.

Respecting our past brings peace to our hearts and minds. Our thoughts become clearer. People generally have two relations with their past. Either they run from it or they run towards it. People who had difficult pasts feel that running way is the answer. The further they run, the closer it seems. It's our past. We can't run, we can't hide from it. Once we acknowledge and respect our past, it settles down. It gives us the freedom to move on.

People who love to linger in their pasts, who find everything was rosy and better back then, are racing toward the horizon. It's visible, it's there, but it can't be reached. They too, need to understand and respect their past, so they can move on. They must let it go. They must leave the past in the past.

Grab your pen and paper and write down everything that comes to mind when you think about your past. Title the page, "In the Past," and then once you are done, split the list into two parts, good memories and bad memories. Categorise the memories you have just written under each category. Now go through the list under each category and try to understand what lessons you have learnt from each good experiences and each bad experience. Next, try to relate each lesson to an effect on your present.

You will feel a eureka moment when you realise how much your past has impacted your present. How your strengths or limitations have stemmed from your past. How your previous experiences have shaped your vision of yourself and world. This knowledge will bring you a higher understanding of yourself and provide closure.

STEP 2 - THE PRESENT IS A VANTAGE POINT

Once you make peace with your past, you need to accept your present. Accept your present, as you are, what you are. Your present could be better than your expectations, or it could be worse that your dreams, or it could be just another thing you're going through. Whatever it is, it's your present. You need to take count of it. You need to accept it, in its true current self. You need to stop misleading yourself, stop projecting false image to yourself, you need to start acknowledging your present.

Your present is very important, as it carries the seeds from your past and potential fruits for your future. The present is a perfect amalgamation of your past and your future. We can't close our eyes and say that everything is fine, especially when things are clearly not. At the same time, we can't keep complaining about our present, when it's clearly better than our past.

We need to accept it and understand that we are at the point we were supposed to be. The things you have achieved, the milestones you have crossed, the dreams you have fulfilled are all important. Give yourself credit for what you've done in the past and accept your present.

It's a pivot point in your journey. A vantage point, showing you both the trails of your past and the direction for your future. You need to accept it and start living in your present. The past is history. Leave it in peace. The future is what you will create. In time, you will reach it. Today, you are in your present. You need to take stock of your life now and enjoy every moment you have today. There could be lots of challenges, but there is always a silver lining. You need to acknowledge both and accept your present as a gift from your past.

Now, reach back to your pen and paper to write down about your present. Title your new sheet of paper, "Today I Am," and write about your current state. Are you happy in life? How you are doing health wise, career wise, financially? How are your relationships? Try to write as holistically about your present self as you can.

By freely expressing your present feelings, you will understand your true state. For example, you might be going through a phase where you have lost motivation in your work. By writing down your feelings, you might discover that your feeling of emptiness in your current line of work is the reason behind lack of motivation. When you write down your feelings, you open the doors to self-understanding and better decision-making.

STEP 3 - THE FUTURE TO BE

Once you have given due respect to your past and accepted your present, you need to take responsibility for your future.

Your future is one thing that solely depends upon you. Very soon, it will become your present and eventually your past. If you want to have a happier past, you need to create a happier future. It's all in your hands. Tomorrow, you can't blame the stars, or circumstances, or other people. It's you who must manage everything to create the future you desire. You are the master of your life's own ship.

To create a better future, we must shed our fears, limitations, perceptions, prejudices, and accept the full responsibility of shaping and creating it. We must accept that what happened has happened, but what will happen will depend upon us. Our thoughts and our actions will shape the future. The situations, the circumstances, and the challenges are just particles of time. They will come and go. But the responsibility for our future always stays with us.

Once you understand that you are in charge, that your life's ship is steered by your instincts and powered by your determination, you will reach the distant shores you crave. The rough seas and the gusty winds will just be phases of the journey. Whether or not you reach shore depends on you. You are the creator of your future. You can't shy away from this responsibility. If you do not shoulder this responsibility, no one will. Your journey will end in limbo and the destination will never be reached. You are responsible for creating it or destroying it.

Having faith in the future that you can create, that you will create, will open your mind to all the unknown and unforeseen opportunities in front of you. The opportunities will drive you towards your goal. You can choose to waste your life by ignoring this fact, or you can become what you desire. At the end of the day, it's your choice. You will be what you choose to be.

Now take a pen and a new sheet of paper. Title the page, "My Future Will Be," and then write what you want your future to be. Express your vision and write down your thoughts. Think freely, without any restrictions. Again, avoid judging yourself and your thoughts. Don't think about what's possible and what's not. Just spend some time writing the best version of your future.

Putting your future goals on paper does two things. Firstly, it builds your connection with your future self. Secondly, it allows you to see your future more clearly. You will understand your priorities. It gives you a focus. It makes it personal.

Discovering and accepting yourself, your life, your past, present, and your future will guide you as you journey through life. You can't control your past, but you can surely create your future. The present is a confluence of current events. You must make a choice, to look back or to look forward. Your choice will determine your upcoming present. The past is nothing but a reflection of time; both your present and future have been consumed by the past.

At this point, you will have seven sheets titled as follows: The Fears, The Limitations, My Strengths, My Dreams, The Past, Today I Am, and My Future Will Be. These sheets will hold knowledge which reflects who you truly are, inside and out. The curtains of ego and masks of pretension will be taken off. Done diligently, these sheets will show you a pure picture of yourself.

Being a chosen one, who has decided to listen to his internal voice and is willing to set out on the journey to create your ideal future, you have to accept yourself as you are, and the three phases of your life time. This will bring peace to your past and present, while setting you on a journey to create your ideal future.

———

STAGE TWO - CREATION

SINCE LIFE BEGAN, we have been mesmerized by our universe, curious as to its origin story. We have always tried to understand how everything was created and who, if anyone, was behind it. Creation brings life to your dreams. Creation is the expression of your thoughts. Creation can last long after you're gone. Without creation, your hopes and dreams are just random thoughts lost to the seas of time.

Our life is a journey of creation. We create our own world, our own lives. Likewise, we create our own future, present, and past. It's the act of creation that gives meaning to our lives. It's the mark of our existence. And what's a better thing to create than your own dream.

People who did not pursue their dreams or create their ideal futures die with regret The graveyard is a stock room of the greatest innovations, solutions, and ideas which were never shared, expressed, or implemented. It's the irony of structured human society; we raise generations filled with doubts and who always try to be cautious of their own thoughts and actions. Generations burdened with the responsibility to pursue the beaten path and waste their lives doing what others have done.

Creation is an act that makes humans race superior to other known life forms on earth. It's creation that differentiates us from the king of the jungle and the mammoths of the sea. Creation is essential to human existence. It's through the act of creation that our civilization has history. Through the act of creation, we have been able to explore the wonders of the universe and depths of the oceans. Creation has laid the foundation for our future.

Most people are very selfish when it comes to creation. They focus on creating a great life for themselves, for their family members, and sometimes for their friends. Very rarely do we focus on creating something for others; those we care for are automatically considered cared for. They don't understand that nature functions like a stack of dominos. It's an echo chamber. The good deeds you do for others will result in good deeds in your own life. This does not mean that you need to spend money on others. Sharing knowledge is also a way to pay it forward and help someone else learn the tools of self-reliance.

Creating your dreams is also your responsibility. You will be creating throughout your life. If not for yourself, then for others. It's the most intimate part of human evolution. We create things. We bring things to life. Your dreams, your desires are important. You must put in effort to bring them to life. You must strive to create your world.

Dreaming about how things should be or how they have been is of no use. It's a futile mental exercise. You reach nowhere. You can spend hours, days, weeks, months, even years dreaming about how your life should be and how your future should be. But if you don't take effort to create it, nothing will happen. You will be where you are or may be even lower.

Time will keep moving; you can use it to create your reality or do nothing. Both options and results will be yours to own. Nature communicate to us in subtle ways. When you do not take action to create a better future, it understands you are happy the way you are. It considers your lack of action as your acceptance of the current situation. It understands you don't want to grow further. It understands you have reached your pinnacle. And then it stops to support you. And the only way from the pinnacle, is downwards.

On the other side, when you start taking action for creating the future you wish to have, nature supports you. There are hardly few things more satisfying in the world than to see your dreams coming to life. To achieve your goals. To be what you wanted to be. It's all in your hands and in your willingness to progress towards your goal, one step a time.

Whatever you desire, a high-paying job, a bigger house, a newer car, a healthier body, a committed relationship, fatter bank balance, it's all within your grasps. Your future will be what you want it to be. All you have to do is take actions to create it. If you want to be traveler, travel the world. If you want to be an explorer, explore the world. You decide; it's completely your choice.

People have the desire and the will to create their ideal future. But they rarely make up their mind. The heart tells them one thing and then logic tells them another. This is paradox of the ages. It becomes extremely difficult to choose from seemingly two great options. But the choice must be made, and you must decide which path to follow. It's your journey, so it should be your decision. Consult with as many people as you wish, read, research, study to a great extent. But in the end, you must take a call and start your journey towards future you wish to create.

PART A - FOLLOW YOUR INSTINCTS

In the beginning, it becomes very difficult. The years of repetitive thinking, the logical arguments, societal pressure. Everything seems designed to stop you. But you need to have faith in your instincts. Afterall you are embodiment of millions of years of evolution. Your inner self knows more than you can imagine; it will guide you to the right path. If you can't take bigger steps, take baby steps. Every iota of movement towards your goal, will give you more confidence in yourself. Sometimes, we freeze by our own thoughts. We create our own imaginative demons, obstacles and challenges. It's in this moment of choice between fear and freedom that you need to follow your heart. You need to follow your instinct.

Everything starts with a decision. Once you chose the freedom to create your own world, the whole world falls into place. That's when everything starts making sense. That's when you will get the focus and direction. The decision mutes all the noise of doubts in your head. The fear subsides and the seeds of freedom sprouts. Have faith in your capabilities and you will reach the goal.

Your dream is your journey. You might not know yet where it will end, but surely your inner voice will give you direction from time to time. Many things you think as of now as final, might only be a milestone of your journey. It's absolutely fine, to progress from milestone to a milestone. In the end, you will be able to see the chart of your journey and feel proud that you decided and took the right steps. Every milestone will represent your belief in yourself, your passion for progress and your determination to proceed further.

The always present discontent within oneself, is the indication that something needs to be changed. Something needs to be improved. Some landscapes to be explored. Don't silence it. Give it a flame and let it guide you where you should be. We have finite lifetime, but the opportunities are infinite. We must capitalise on these opportunities; we must bring our dreams to life. It's only you, who can do it.

Self-doubt, pessimism, or fear of failure are just the small hurdles testing your commitment. These hurdles are created by your own mind to judge your sincerity towards your future. It's just a mind game to check and test you. Once you start moving the right direction, your mind must pull in all the resources from different parts of our brains. It has to work overtime and give solutions, as flashes of light, which you don't even know exists. So, it's justifiable that your mind tests you.

But once you cross the self-testing hurdles, the whole world of opportunities opens towards you. You will be able to see the solutions, which you never looked at. All these things were there before as well, but you were not seeking them. You were not looking. Now you want them, hence you will find them. Your mind will be focused. You will get the resources to pave the way towards your goal.

At the same time, you must realise our mind is a hyperactive machine. It's always busy with something. With some thoughts. There is always a commotion in our mind. So, if you want it to focus on your dream, you need to tell it and push yourself towards it. Your actions will show your intentions, which your mind will understand and start to support you. If you don't take action, nothing will happen. The mind will focus back on its own commotion.

Now refer back to sheets titled, "My Dreams" and "My Future Will Be." Go through the list. Afterwards, close your eyes and pick any one dream you would like to pursue now. Don't be judgmental. Let your instincts choose it. For example, if out of all the listed dreams, speaking foreign language excites you, pick it. Don't worry about whether it will help your finances, or career or health or relationships or how you will learn it, etc. Don't worry about anything and just pick it, let your instincts lead you. Once you have a chosen dream with you, write it on paper and move to next part.

PART B - LIVE NOW, ACT NOW

Initially we start with doubts and enthusiasm, then we slow down. As our soul find the solace in our actions, we get comfortable and slow down our pace. Then the slowdown become procrastination and in time we fall back into the trap, where we were before we started. The solution to maintaining the journey of creation is understanding the importance of now.

Now is a powerful tool in the hands of creators. Now is an attitude of the winner. Now is the slayer of the procrastination and laziness. Now is the anecdote against the doubts about the results of your actions. Now is the invisible hand which will keep holding you from falling back into the trap of mundane life. Now is the biggest friend in your journey of creating your future.

Once you have decided to create your world, you must act now. No thought, no decision, no action should be postponed. Delays are deadly. The window of opportunity is always open for a limited time. You must act now. Now is a rule of survival; now is the rule of the winners. Don't delay any action that could lead you to your goal.

Act now but have patience for your rewards. Between efforts and rewards, the one thing you have more control is efforts. So put in your efforts, act now. Rewards will come in time. It's like, if you need a fruit in future, you need to plant the seed now. If you fail to act now, you will fail to have fruit in the future.

Many people have ambitious dreams, and gigantic plans.

But they all fail to simple factor of not acting fast. They delay, they want to play it safe. They wait and watch and become relic in time. Time waits for no one. If you have a dreams, if you have a plan, if you have a solution, you must implement it now. Postponing is a recipe for failure.

The only thing more important than actions itself is speed of action. Speed matters. The business idea you have, could be similar to what others have also thought of. The only thing that will give you an edge is your timely action. The promotion that you seek, will be sought by plenty of other people, so if you delay your progress towards it, you won't stand a chance.

We waste so many years of our life thinking we have time to do what we want to do. But we don't realise, our life is limited. It's our choice to squander a bigger percentage postponing the future we want or more time living it. The more we delay taking action, the lesser time we will get to enjoy our real self. The more we delay, the higher regrets we will have. We must act now. The world is not going to wait for us. It's like survival instinct. The fastest wins.

Now get yourself a pen and paper to work on your selected dream. On the top the sheet, write the dream, like "learn a new language." Now make a list of five things that you must do in next 24 hours to fulfill your dream. For example, selection of language, enrolling for the online classes, buying books, making a three months learning schedule, writing a list of people you will learn from informally.

Once you are done with the first dream, then follow the same process with the next and then another. It's about putting yourself into the cycle of fulfilling your dreams. Dream by dream, step by step, you will create your future.

Carving your own path and creating your own future is a manifestation of humankind's superiority. Not every living thing on this planet gets this opportunity. Despite their amazing skills, most of their life is about survival. You are better than them. You have the power of choice. You must exercise it. This will bring peace to your soul and in the end, you will be able to depart with fewer regrets.

Don't hold your life in abeyance. Don't delay your future. Don't berate yourself to a life of self-pity and misery. You are better than what you think. You are stronger than what you believe. You are smarter than your thoughts. Don't restrain yourself. Set yourself free and live a spectacular life.

———

STAGE THREE - EMBRACE THE JOURNEY

ONCE YOU SET on the path, you will face many internal and external challenges. Out of the two, the difficult ones are the internal challenges. There will be many battles fought within your mind. Battles which no one will witness, no one will hear. It is only you versus your mind. After each battle you will become stronger. You will emerge better and closer to your goal.

Embracing the journey will give you strength to carry on and make you resilient. Starting up is important but keep going despite every challenge, is essential. Persistence pays. The perseverance you will gain after winning internal battles will become your shield and your weapon to external challenges.

As we proceed towards our goal, just like our mind checks our intentions, the nature also checks us. It places small hurdles for us to overcome. Each hurdle or challenge teaches us new things. It's nature's way of teachings. That's how it prepares us for the next steps. That's how it helps us to develop new strengths.

Amazing things start happening once we start winning

these battles. With each battle, we learn new skills. We learn new realities. We learn new limits. Hence, we shall always celebrate and appreciate ourselves for winnings these battles. All the praise and celebrations shall not be held for the final outcome. We shall celebrate as we proceed. Every victory is important.

PART A - BE ORIGINAL

Once you start your own journey, it's always tempting see how others have achieved their goals. Which path they followed for their journey. Which resources they had and which resources they acquired. The seed of self-comparison, or as called incorporates, benchmarking, is a notional concept, which will only make you a replica of someone else. Your journey will end as someone else's journey.

It is tempting to idolise someone. To have a hero. To position someone as your future self. Many people live in this illusion. But it's just a fruitless journey. Even if you manage to reach to become just like your idol, you will be empty inside. You will be dissatisfied. You will be impatient. Because, you couldn't become what you should have, instead someone else.

Never aspire to be just like someone else. Every, person has his own journey and you would never have a true idea, what's their journey about. So instead of putting in years of efforts to imitate someone else, put in efforts to become yourself. Your instinct already knows what you should be and what you can be. All you have to do is follow it. Others followed their journey; you must follow your own.

Imagine a world where everyone aspires to be like someone else; eventually, there is no protagonist. As every individiaul is just like everyone else. There will be no innovation. There will be no progress. There will be no breakthroughs. All that will exist is a dull, gray existence. There will be no one to think beyond what others have achieve. There will be no one to explore the unexplored. There will be no one to test the untested. The growth of the whole civilization will come to a halt and then decline.

Every person, corporation, or nation, progresses on their own journey. They use the available resources to them. They find solutions to their problems. They create their own future. The end objective could be the same, but the paths will always be different. Two people taking same path will also generate different results. You can copy other people's actions, but you can't copy others mind. No two minds are the same. No two legends are the same. So, how can there be two of you?

So, you must be your own star, your own light. You must lead your own way. It's your journey, it's your future. You must embrace the journey to create your future. Journey to realise and fulfill your potential. Journey to discover yourself. Journey to step beyond your fears. Journey to be, what you were meant to be.

When you are creating your own path, you are actually showing the way to thousands of other aspirants, who are sittings on the fence, pondering to either stop fearing and start living or fall back to the comfortable routine. The originality is always impressive. It always stands out. Being original is like being rare, as you will be only one of your kind. No one else was or will be like you. People will aspire to be you, but they can't. They can have similar success, but they will always be your shadow.

Also, when you aspire for originality, it's opens thousands of new doors. As there is nothing to follow, so you chose the path you like and chart the course of your own journey. Isn't it real freedom? Just to be how you want to be. No roads to follow, no rules to observe, no limitation to honor. Just complete freedom to chalk out the path and lay foundation for others.

PART B - HARD WORK IS SUPREME

As we are an intelligent race, we try to use this gift in finding shortcuts to reach our goals faster and easier way. We try to trick nature and skip few lessons. Sometimes we do reach the goal and create the life we want. But that's nature's trick and consequently all the success earned is short lived. There is no replacement for plain and simple hard work. No matter what the world tries to preach to you, always remember there are no shortcuts to success. There is no replacement for hard work. Hard work itself is a supreme form of dedication towards creating your future life.

When you become the chosen one and pursuing your journey; your mind, your body, your acquaintances will try to trick you into this false trap of lazy living. Promoting short term solutions is a smart approach. But do remember, a quick fix also breaks quickly. It's only for short time. But the future you are creating is not for a short time. It's where you will live for the rest of your life. So, we should think twice before opting for quick fixes.

You must work hard and complement it with your intelligence. This combination is more than enough to get you where you want to be. The journey of miles is completed one step at a time, taken in sequence. Staying persistent and focused is the greatest weapon in the arsenal of the winner. You have already decided to walk on this path. Keep walking, keep moving, keep progressing.

The journey you will be pursuing will take you where you wish to be. It will create the world that you want to create. We humans enjoy journey as equally as destination. Enjoy the journey towards your destination. You will cross through this road only once. So, make the best of each passing moment. These people, these opportunities, these challenges may not come again. So, make the very best of each experience. It's your journey and one day, you will have great story to tell.

Another benefit of working hard to overcome obstacles is that you will understand the importance of each challenge and you will recognise each opportunity far before anyone could imagine. You will understand the pattern. You will see the relationship between challenges and rewards. You will know what rewards await you beyond your current challenges. You will focus on the rewards and the challenges will become just a mist covering your view. You will know, beyond the curtain of challenges, lays a land that awaits you.

You will know that it's a game. Every step you take will gain you points and the more steps you take, the more challenges you face, the more options you explore, you will be getting closer towards the top. You will enjoy the process and you will want it more.

There will be times, when quitting seems like a better option. When the challenge will be so big, and you can't think of a solution. There will be moments when you will self-doubt yourself. You will question if you really need to reach the end. You will doubt your capabilities. You will fear the pain you will get if you go against the challenge. Giving up will seems like your only choice. But you know, you will still make it. You know why, because you refused to give in. Because you will know, giving in now, is comfortable for a while, but the pain will last forever. You will know, it's either creating your dream or living someone else. You will know, it's either life of freedom or life of fear. You will know, with hard work you will overcome any mountain.

People will keep looking at their past and wonder, why it's like that and hope their future will be better. But little do they know, it's the future which becomes the past. Our past represents, our reactions to our challenges. Today, when you choose comfort or quick fix our hard work, tomorrow you will look back and wonder why it happened. People will pin their hopes on tomorrow and again give in to today's challenges. Little they understand, it's today that determines your future and create your past. It's today, when the choices of giving in or keep going needs to be made. It's always, today. Tomorrow will change based on what you do today. Tomorrow will mere reflect the choices you will make today. It's today you need to focus and give your hundred percent effort. Because now is the time to create your future.

When you are surrounded by fears, when negative thoughts have casted shadow on you, when doubts drag you down, have faith in yourself. Your faith in yourself is one of your greatest armour. Have faith in your abilities to create what you set to create, have faith in your intelligence to make a better judgements. Have faith in your instincts to guide you in the right direction. Have faith in your tenacity, dedication and strong will. Just a little bit of faith in yourself is all you need. It will give you tremendous amount of courage to carry on.

When you fall in the trap of self-pity and criticism, always remember who you are. You are not a particle of the sand, who will be moved from place to place on the whims and wishes of the wind. You represent an evolution of human civilization. You hold the knowledge and experience of your ancestors. You are the chosen one, who has decided to tread on the unknown path. You are the courageous one, who will conquer beyond anyone's dreams. You are a legend in making. The current challenges are just small pebbles in your journey. You can step over them, as and when you wish.

Sometimes, your mind will play games. It will say you have come a long way, now you can relax. It will say you are much better than before. It will say you have done a lot. It will say you are now much better than others. It will say you to settle down and relax. The only way to avoid this trap, is to focus on the action. Your actions need to guide your mind. Your efforts, your actions, have greater control on your mind. You need to work diligently and accordingly; your mind will follow your lead.

With your hard work and perseverance, as you keep on progressing in your journey the stronger you will become. The mind won't be able to play games with you. The voices of others will not reach your core. The challenges will become just a routine. You will attain a higher ground as compare to other mortals. You will see light, when others see darkness. You will fly high, when others fear the storm. You will become yourself, while others will waste their lives to be nothing.

Embracing the journey by carving our own path and working hard to materialise our dreams, gives us a singularity of purpose. It guides us through the deepest forests of doubts. It shows us light in darkest night of fear. It carries us through the longest journey of our lives.

When you are on the journey to create your true self, there will be lot of naysayers. There will be lot of questions, there will be lots of doubts. The obstacle in front of you will look insurmountable. When you reach this point, take a step back and change your focus to your dream. Feel how close you have come to realise it. How far you have come from the starting point. How real is your dream? The focus on the end will help you to cope with the current small obstacles, which will later just become your milestones. Always remember it's your future and with your perseverance you will create it.

Many times, while heading towards our dream, we stumble, we fall, we fail. The pain from these experiences are excruciating. It can break your will. It can erase years of efforts. It can turn you into dust. But you must remember, all these are experiences on your journey. They are just temporary. You cannot give up your life's dream for these temporary disappointments. These failures will come and go. You must keep moving forward. If one approach doesn't work, use another. Every door has a key. You just need to find the right one. And, you will.

You have a dream, you want to create your life, you want to be the person you want to be, so you must embrace the challenges and opportunities of the journey. You should enjoy the process. You must believe your future depends upon you. It's all in your hands. You have the skills, you have the intelligence, and you have the perseverance. You are the chosen one. You will create your life, the way you want it.

———

LIVING A BETTER LIFE

IF YOU OBSERVE a bird hatching out of the egg, you will realise, the nature wants us to be self-reliant. The experience, the effort, the process of breaking out of the egg, gives strength to the bird to survive. It's that journey, which give strength to their wings to fly over miles of distance. If you break the egg and take out the bird, probably it will never fly and fall prey to other predators very soon. Likewise, nature wants us to be self-reliant and break out of our mould. The mould we think is our entire universe and our life.

If a newborn bird can rely on itself to break out of the shell, you are much better to break out of your shell. Your fears, your doubts, your thoughts can't stop you from spreading your wings and flying off to the future you wanted. It's your dream. Nothing is going to stop you from achieving it.

When you rely on yourself to create your future, you will have lots of reactions from everyone around you. Your act of self-reliance is act of freedom. Its act of refusing to follow the beaten path. It's an act of hope for a better life. You will become focal point of attention. They will watch you, talk about you, they will despise you, they will love you. They don't know how to regard you. Their hearts will tell them to hold you in reverence and their mind will tell to treat you with indifference. Whatever they do, they won't be able to ignore you.

People with open hearts and minds will start respecting you. They know, if you want something, you will go for it, with or without their help. They will know, you are not a dreamer but a creator. People hold the creator in the highest respect. They know, not everyone has the courage to create their future. They themselves have given in to their fears and abandoned their own journey. So, they want to be part of your journey. They will seek solace in your achievements. They will look up to you and deep in their hearts, hold you in the highest esteem. They will treat you with a reverence.

Your family and friends will be surprised and shocked by the rise of your flight. They would like to see you fly even higher, go beyond the visible sky and reach for the stars. They will try to support you at every step of your journey. They would love to play their own little part and help you in creating your dream.

There will be watchers who will not know how to react. Who will not know what to do. Who will be so encompassed by their own little thinking that they will fail to see the bigger picture. These people are the lost wanderers. You shall try to support and guide them, by simply being yourself. Soon or later, they will see the brighter side of your journey and stand up to cheer you.

You will shine like a beacon of hope to world lost in the sea of rationalizations, thoughts, customs, traditions, cultures, fears and self-doubts. You will be the ray of hope for the ones who have given in to their struggle. You will become a paragon of human progress. Looking at you, they will believe in the future. They will know, we can create our own world. They will understand the power of creation is within us. They will look into the future and the millions of possibilities it can bring.

Self-reliance hold the key to our future. It's the answer to all our challenges. It's the solution to all our problems. It's the greatest form of respect one can give to his live. Its freedom from seeking external motivation. Its freedom from having false expectations from others. Its freedom from the pain of relying on someone else for your future. It's a mindset of a creator.

By becoming self-reliant, you also become a support system for others. People will look up to you. They will know, if anyone could do it, it's you. You will not be part of the whiners, who will simply cry for everything they don't have and blame the world. They will not take initiative to do it themselves but expect the world to serve everything to them on a golden plate. They are grownups, who still behave and act like small babies. Their mind is still the same. The bodies might have changed the shape, but the mind has not grown much.

Self-reliance will change your life forever. You would not be the same person as before. You will not be stuck in the day to day routine. You will not be just another face in the crowd. You will not be going to your death bed with heart full of regrets. You will be the chosen one, who made a choice, listen to his heart and believed in his capability to create his own future. Your life will be a diamond among the coal. You will live among others, but your shine will overshadow everything.

The time will change. The innovations and inventions will come and go. But the true genius will have his shadow casted on the centuries to come. The power of originality. That's how important it is to be yourself. The legacy you will create will impact many centuries. Your journey to realize your dreams is not only yours but for the generations to come. The choices you make today will have a lasting impact on the future.

Self-reliance gives us the courage to chase our vision. It makes us confident. It makes us reliable. It makes us, visionary. As we rely on ourselves and know we can do it, so we strive harder. We don't look up to others to solve our problem. We don't expect world to create our vision. We believe it's all in our hands and we must do.

Self-reliance also bring responsibility. It's not only about creating things for ourselves, but also for others. We need to guide others as well. We need to show them the importance and power of self-reliance. We need to show them the way out of their daily struggles. We need to hold their hands and take them on path of freedom. We need to remind them; they are the creator of their future. Whatever they dream, they can realise it. They need to have faith in their capabilities and listen to their internal voice. They too can become great. They too can become legend. They too can become free.

Self-reliance is an alchemist we look for. It's an elixir we crave for. It's a panacea we all seek. It's a highest praise we can offer to our creator. It's the way of not only showing, but also realising our own capabilities. It's how we will get to know, what we can do. It's how we will show the way to our future generations to realise their dreams. It's a how we will set on a journey to create the world we want to live in. It's the hope we all need. So, set on the journey of creating your own dreams and have faith in self-reliance. You will reach the stars.

Just like the old Sidr tree, standing tall in the middle of a desert, you will also stand tall despite your challenges. You will also stand above the crowd. You will also become an exception to the norms. You will become the protagonist you been looking for. It's one short life. Create it and live it, the way it should be. You have all the resources, knowledge, and vision required. All you must do is, listen to your inner voice and rely on yourself. It's your future and you are the creator.

———

In support of:

MENTAL HEALTH FOUNDATION

Mental Health Foundation is the UK's charity for everyone's mental health. With prevention at the heart of what we do, we aim to find and address the sources of mental health problems.

We invite you to join us.
www.mentalhealth.org.uk

FAMOUS FIREFLY

It's an initiative to drive change in the mindset towards emotional well-being. We create awareness, educate professionals and collaborate with like-minded people to build healthier & a better world.

Join us on Instagram & Twitter - @famousfirefly, or learn more about us at www.famousfirefly.com

ABOUT THE AUTHOR

Sukhpreet is a qualified economist and marketing expert, who has spent the past 15 years working as a Senior-level Executive with Fortune 500 companies.

Having personally seen brilliant professionals succumbing to stress, anxiety, and even depression, he has set on a pursuit to address this epidemic. He believes that individuals, organizations, and society must come together to address this challenge.

He would like to listen to your thoughts and experiences. You can reach him at sukhpreet@famousfirefly.com or join him on Instagram & Twitter - @sukhpreet_ace.

44575060R00040

Printed in Poland
by Amazon Fulfillment
Poland Sp. z o.o., Wrocław